S

FREMONT UNIFIED SCHOOL DISTRICT
Fremont, California
ESEA 1966-67

MAGELLAN

FIRST AROUND THE WORLD

MAGELLAN

FIRST AROUND THE WORLD

By RONALD SYME

Illustrated by William Stobbs

WILLIAM MORROW & COMPANY · NEW YORK · 1953

 Published simultaneously in the Dominion of Canada by George J. McLeod Limited, Toronto. Library of Congress Catalog Card Number: 53-7102.

••••••••••

Also by Ronald Syme

BAY OF THE NORTH

CORTES OF MEXICO

CHAMPLAIN OF THE ST. LAWRENCE

COLUMBUS, FINDER OF THE NEW WORLD

LA SALLE OF THE MISSISSIPPI

The king's palace in Lisbon stood on a grassy hillside above the river, surrounded by a garden with a low stone wall. A slender dark-haired boy often came to sit on this wall, to look down at the ships in the river far below.

Ferdinand Magellan had been in Lisbon for only a few months. Until he was thirteen years old, he had lived with his family among the gentle hills of northern Portugal.

Then one day his father had sent for him. "My

son," he said, "now you must go to the royal palace in Lisbon to begin your education. You will learn good manners there and many other things besides. You will meet famous people—artists and poets, generals and wise teachers. You will become one of His Majesty's faithful attendants."

Ferdinand hated leaving his home. Lisbon seemed to him a large and unfriendly city when he arrived there. But he soon discovered that from the palace garden he could see the distant ocean. It was Magellan's first glimpse of the sea and the ships that sailed it.

All Portugal and Spain were concerned with those ships in the year 1493. Explorers were making fresh discoveries every day. Christopher Columbus was just back from his first voyage across the Atlantic Ocean. Men had always believed that any ship crossing the Atlantic would fall over the edge of the world. Now the amazing news of an unknown continent on the other side of the ocean was traveling through Europe like wildfire.

Young Magellan kept thinking about that voyage of Columbus's. He began to wonder if the world might not be larger than most people supposed. He knew that a sea captain named Bartholomew Diaz had sailed all the way to the southern tip of Africa six years before, but no ship had ever gone beyond that point. Perhaps other countries lay somewhere farther on in that direction.

"Do you think a ship could reach India by going around Africa?" Magellan asked one of the king's geographers.

"What a strange idea!" the man exclaimed. "And even if it were possible, what would be the use of such a voyage? Silks and spices and gold from India reach us quite well as it is. They are brought by Arab ships to the coast of Arabia. Camels carry them across the desert to the shores of the Mediterranean Sea. There they are loaded into Italian vessels and are brought here to Lisbon."

"But if a Portuguese ship could sail all the way to India," said Magellan, "she could bring the goods straight back to Lisbon. It would be much quicker and safer than the present journey."

As Magellan grew older, his curiosity about the unknown parts of the world continued. When he was nineteen, a rumor reached Lisbon which doubled his interest in voyages of discovery. It was reported that a Portuguese sea captain, Vasco da Gama, had sailed around the southern tip of Africa, that his four little ships had then crossed an unknown ocean and had actually arrived at the port of Calicut on the coast of India.

Da Gama returned to Portugal in 1499. He had been away for two years. He had lost three of his four ships during the 24,000-mile voyage. Sixty of his one hundred and seventy men had died. But he had reached India! As Magellan had suspected, it actually was possible to get to India by sailing around Africa.

Magellan listened eagerly to the stories told by the seamen who had been with Vasco da Gama. He heard about churches built of gleaming copper and

golden statues with priceless rubies for eyes. He learned that the king of Calicut lived in a splendid palace, surrounded by white-robed servants and men in strange armor. Peacocks strutted on white marble terraces around the palace. Calicut's harbor was full of little ships. These were the vessels which brought the spices and gold and silks to Arabia.

Young Magellan watched with fascination while the maps in the king's library were changed by the court geographers to include the information Da Gama had brought back. Now those maps could show for the first time the great ocean on the eastern shores of Africa.

Day after day Magellan watched the ships pass along the river below the palace. He saw them raise anchor and disappear toward the sea. He sniffed the fragrant cargoes they brought from India—barrels of cloves and cinnamon, nutmeg and ginger. The shops in Lisbon were filled with golden necklaces and diamonds and silverware. All these goods had come from India in Portuguese ships.

Two years later, news came of further exciting discoveries. Amerigo Vespucci, who had already given his name to the American continent, was exploring the coast of Brazil. Portuguese captains had sailed along the coast of East Africa. More and more ships were coming and going in the river at Lisbon. Magellan longed to sail in one of them, and to have some part in one of these exciting voyages of discovery.

In 1504, Vasco da Gama was ordered by the king of Portugal to return to India and builds forts and warehouses on the coast. His headquarters were to be at a port named Cochin, which lay south of Calicut.

Da Gama collected a fleet of twenty-one ships. Fifteen hundred soldiers were recruited, and everyone in Portugal was talking about this great new adventure.

One day Magellan left the palace garden. He walked down the road to the quays beside the river. There he met a group of officers from Da Gama's ships and told them he wanted to sail with the fleet.

The men looked at him. "But you are not a sailor," they said doubtfully. "You know nothing about ships and the sea. How could a fine young gentleman like you be useful? We need only seamen now."

"Then I will *be* one," said Magellan. "For eleven years I have longed to see the world."

When Vasco da Gama's fleet sailed in the autumn

of 1504, Ferdinand Magellan went with it. He was twenty-four years old and on his way at last to strange oceans and stranger lands. Instead of the rich velvet clothing of a courtier, he wore a rough jersey and baggy knee breeches. Happily he set about learning to wash down the decks and to paint the ship's timbers with tar.

Magellan stood in the bow of the ship, gazing at the shore they were approaching. Splendid trees covered with scarlet flowers grew along it. A city with white walls and flat roofs stood a little way inland.

Da Gama's fleet had reached India. The king of Cochin was already coming to greet the Portuguese ships, riding in a golden litter strapped to the back of an elephant. Behind him came warriors in armor. Trumpets were blowing and drums were beating. The people of Cochin were pouring out of the town and hurrying toward the beach.

During the next few months, Magellan explored the Indian city. He wandered through crowded and noisy bazaars. He sat in gardens where fountains glittered and monkeys leaped among the branches above his head. And he still wondered about the unknown parts of the world.

The king of Calicut became jealous of the Portuguese and sent a fleet of over two hundred vessels to attack them in Cochin. Most of the Portuguese ships had already gone back to Lisbon. Only eleven vessels were still in the harbor.

Magellan was soon fighting his first battle. His

own ship was attacked by fifty small enemy vessels, and hundreds of natives climbed onto the deck. For six hours Magellan and his companions fought with swords and daggers, and finally they drove the attackers over the side. The enemy fleet was beaten and sailed back to Calicut. Magellan had been wounded in the shoulder, where a blow from a sword had cut through his armor.

Gradually the Portuguese in Cochin began to hear of great countries which lay still farther toward the east. Da Gama ordered a captain named Diego Sequeira to take five ships and find out if these stories were true.

Sequeira appointed Magellan to command one of the vessels, and the voyage began in September, 1509. The ships sailed south to Ceylon and then turned east, straight into the sunrise.

Some weeks later, Magellan and his companions reached Malaya; they were the first Europeans to see it. Eagerly Magellan asked himself what country might lie beyond Malaya. Or was there perhaps a

great ocean that lay still farther toward the east?

Another thought entered his mind. Men said the world was round. Could anyone reach Malaya by sailing westward from Portugal across the Atlantic Ocean, as Columbus had done? Such a voyage might be shorter than the one around Africa and across the Indian Ocean.

Sequeira's vessels anchored close to the Malayan town of Malacca. The harbor was crowded with strange ships. Magellan stared curiously at square-sailed junks from China and Arab dhows from the Red Sea, with their queer slanted masts and triangular sails. Clumsy Indian vessels like wooden fortresses floated nearby. Tiny-sailed East Indian canoes darted across the bay.

Magellan soon heard rumors of large islands lying in brilliant blue seas somewhere to the east. He listened to brown-faced natives speaking unknown languages. A great longing filled his heart to sail on eastward. There were so many things he wanted to know. Who were these mysterious people who

called themselves Chinese? Where did their country lie? What did they mean when they spoke of a country called Nippon (Japan)?

Sudden danger put an end to Magellan's thoughts. The Sultan of Malacca was a treacherous man. He smiled at the Portuguese and allowed them to buy cinnamon and pepper and cloves. Meanwhile, he made plans to murder them.

One afternoon, hundreds of armed natives came pouring into the sheds where the Portuguese seamen were filling sacks with spice. The sailors snatched up cutlasses and knives. Fighting shoulder to shoulder, they retreated slowly toward the quay.

Magellan was on the deck of his ship when the fighting began. "Lower three boats," he ordered. "Fifteen armed men will go in each of them."

The boats reached the shore, where Magellan led his men in a charge along the quay. The natives were driven back, and the Portuguese sailors hastened into the boats. Meanwhile, the guns in the ships opened fire on the town. Iron cannon balls smashed through the houses. The people of Malacca fled in terror. Quickly the Portuguese ships hoisted sail and steered out of the harbor to begin the long voyage back to India.

A few years later, Magellan was given leave to go home to Portugal. Because of his brave conduct, he had been promoted to the rank of captain.

Magellan felt almost sure now that it would be possible to reach Malaya by sailing west from Portugal. He knew that America was on the other side of the Atlantic Ocean. Surely there must be some kind of sea passage through that continent. Perhaps some great river ran across it from east to west.

"Why do you think that there is another ocean west of America?" he was asked.

"The natives of Malaya said a great ocean lay between their country and the sunrise," Magellan replied. "This same ocean may reach to the western shores of America."

"Even if you are right," he was told, "think of

the voyage you would have to make! Across the Atlantic, through the American continent, and then across another ocean. Even if you finally did reach Malaya, you would still have to get back to Portugal. No one could possibly survive such a voyage. You would die of hunger or thirst or shipwreck on the way—or get lost on this great ocean you talk about."

Magellan kept on studying his maps. Now they showed India and the whole coast line of Africa. But on none of them appeared the Pacific Ocean or the western coast of America. The map makers had never heard of such places.

A strange story reached Lisbon a year or so later. A Spanish explorer, Nunez de Balboa, had crossed the Isthmus of Panama. On its farther side he had seen an ocean that stretched to the horizon. He was the first European to sight the Pacific.

"That must be the ocean I heard of," Magellan exclaimed to his friends. "Now I will find a way into it and sail across to Malaya."

"Who will give you the ships and money for such a voyage?" someone asked.

"The king," Magellan replied. "Our country will be able to claim all the islands I discover on the way. We shall build up a wonderful empire in the East. It will bring us fame and great prosperity."

But the king of Portugal laughed at the idea. "No one could sail around the world," he said. "No one could find a way through the American continent. Even the famous Columbus could not do that. I shall give no money for this crazy scheme."

"Then, Your Majesty, I must find others who will," Magellan replied.

Ferdinand Magellan went quietly back to his lodgings. He packed his belongings and left Lisbon. A few days after his thirty-seventh birthday, he reached the Spanish city of Seville. Someone in Spain might be ready to listen to his idea.

Spain's new empire in the West Indies was flourishing by that time, and people in Spain knew that fortunes could be made in unknown parts of the world.

Magellan soon met a man in Seville, an important official in the Spanish government, who listened attentively to his scheme. "Your idea is interesting," he said. "King Charles must hear about it."

Magellan waited impatiently for several months to receive some word from the Spanish king, and at last a message reached him. Six noblemen had formed a committee to consider Magellan's plan, and he was ordered to appear before them.

Magellan faced the six men across a table. He knew that this was the most important moment of his life. He had given up his Portuguese citizenship when he came to Spain, and he had only a little money. If his plan was turned down, he would be penniless in a strange country.

The committee had already found out a great deal about Magellan. They knew that he was the son of an old Portuguese family and that he had been educated at the royal court. They knew that he had

gone to sea as an ordinary sailor and had spent seven years in the East; that he had been wounded in action and promoted for gallantry; that he had commanded his own ship. They knew that he had recently married a Spanish lady.

Magellan talked to the committee for three hours. He told them he was confident that he could find a strait leading across the unknown interior of the American continent.

"When I reach the ocean beyond America," said Magellan, "I will sail across it, no matter how long

the voyage. I am sure, my lords, that I will reach the islands which lie near Malaya. I will claim ownership of them for the king of Spain."

"How long will this voyage take?" asked one of the committee.

"Not more than two years," Magellan replied. "I hope to do it in less, my lord."

The conference went on for several days. At last the committee made their decision. "We approve of your idea," they said to Magellan. "We will recommend it to King Charles."

Another month went by. Then a large sealed letter was brought to Magellan. King Charles had given his permission for the voyage, and Spain would provide five ships for it. The expedition was to start as soon as possible.

Magellan was desperately busy during the next year. The five ships were the *San Antonio*, the *Trinidad*, the *Concepcion*, the *Victoria*, and the *Santiago*. All five needed a complete overhauling. Their rigging and masts must be renewed. Rotten planks in the hulls must be replaced.

Meanwhile, the king of Portugal had heard of Magellan's success in Spain and was intensely jealous. He tried to bribe Magellan to return to Portugal. He wrote letters urging the king of Spain to forbid the voyage. Portuguese spies were sent with plans for damaging the ships. They also had instructions to spread the rumor that the vessels were not fit to go to sea.

There were so many secret enemies around him

that Magellan could trust no one. He had to supervise every detail of the work of repairing the ships and securing supplies for the voyage. Day after day he gave orders, answered questions, listed and checked the necessary stores for each vessel.

"There are no seamen willing to make this dangerous voyage," one officer told him. "They believe the Portuguese story that our ships are rotten."

"Then go to every port in Spain and find men who have not heard it," Magellan replied.

He went on preparing his list. Ten tons of biscuit; 2500 pounds of candles; 89 lanterns; 5 tons of gunpowder; 600 pounds of sugar.

"The carpenters have stopped work," another officer reported. "Portuguese agents are making trouble among them."

Magellan left his cabin and went to see the men. "Go back to your work or get off my ships," he said. "I can hire other carpenters if necessary."

He went on with his planning. Five thousand arrows for the crossbows; 10,500 fishhooks; 40

cartloads of firewood; 2000 pounds of honey; 58 heavy guns; 3 forges and bellows.

Sailors came from all over Spain. Some of them deserted as soon as they heard the frightening stories spread by Magellan's enemies. But others stayed, and gradually the crews were hired and the ships were repaired.

Magellan carried on with his enormous task of securing food and trade goods: 4000 brass and copper bracelets as presents for the natives; 200 colored handkerchiefs; 5000 sheath knives; 1000 mirrors; 200 little red caps; 8 tons of copper; 50 heavy muskets; 1000 lances.

At last the new sails were fitted to the spars. Compasses and charts were stowed away in the cabins. Two hundred and sixty-seven men were ready in the five ships—Spaniards, Portuguese, Italians, Englishmen, and Dutchmen. The last supplies were hurried aboard. Up the gangways came barrels of tar, coils of rope, oil for the lanterns, and tubs of salt.

On a warm, sunny afternoon in September, 1519, Magellan said good-by to his wife and baby son. He hurried back to the quays and stepped on board the *Trinidad*. Trumpets sounded a shrill call.

Thirty-nine-year-old Ferdinand Magellan was starting out on the first attempt ever made to sail around the world.

The five little ships staggered southward in the Atlantic. A gale was screaming across the ocean.

Great white-topped waves towered above the masts of the vessels. Flying spray drenched Magellan as he stood on the *Trinidad's* deck.

Bad weather lasted until the ships reached the equator and turned toward the southwest. Then the wind dropped and the sea became calm. On and on went the ships, sailing eighty, one hundred, one hundred and twenty miles a day. At the end of October they had been at sea for six weeks. Then came trouble.

Every evening the other four ships sailed close to the *Trinidad* to receive orders from Magellan. Captain Cartagena of the *San Antonio* began to be unruly toward his commanding officer, asking him sharp questions about his plans for the voyage.

"Follow the flagship and ask no questions," ordered Magellan. He already suspected that Cartagena had been bribed by the Portuguese to make trouble.

Another week went by. Cartagena became more careless and more impudent. One day Magellan

commanded him to come on board the *Trinidad*.

"I will have no mutiny," said Magellan when Cartagena stood before him. He glanced at a nearby officer. "Take this man away," he said. "He is to be locked up aboard his own ship and he is to be guarded night and day."

On November 29, 1519, the five vessels reached the coast of South America and anchored in a sheltered bay. Natives came swarming down the beach,

carrying hens and potatoes, pineapples and fresh meat. Magellan restocked his ships. He gave one fishhook in exchange for six hens, a mirror for ten fish, a small copper bell for a basket of potatoes. Water casks were refilled and the ships sailed away along the coast toward the south.

On December 13 they reached the bay on which Rio de Janeiro now stands. Magellan believed he was approaching the spot where he hoped to find a channel across the continent. He ordered the ships to keep in sight of the coast and to continue their journey to the south.

Weeks passed and they entered colder seas. The blue sky disappeared and the weather became bitter. Frightful gales caused the ships to stagger and lurch wildly. Magellan gave the order to find shelter. On the last day of March, 1520, the vessels dropped anchor in a little bay near the site of the present town of San Julian. It is down toward the southern end of Argentina, several hundreds of miles from the very tip of South America.

The officers and men were terrified by the bitter cold and wild seas, by the loneliness and desolation of the rocky shore.

The captains of the *San Antonio*, the *Concepcion*, and the *Victoria* consulted together and decided to go no farther. They freed Cartagena from his prison on the *San Antonio*, and he willingly joined in plans for mutiny. So did most of the sailors, and those who refused were promptly put in chains.

The four leaders sent a message to Magellan: "Promise to return at once to Spain and we will follow you. We will go no farther down this miserable coast. Think well before you answer. We hold three ships and have one hundred and seventy men. You have two ships and ninety-seven men."

Magellan sent for the bravest officers and men among those who were still loyal. "Captain Mendoza of the *Victoria* is the leader of these mutineers," he said. "Here is my written reply to him. I am ordering him to surrender and to obey my orders. Go to his ship after dark and give him this letter. If he shows any disobedience, kill him at once. Meanwhile, in another boat, I will send men who will remain hidden under the *Victoria's* stern in the darkness. If you call, they will leap up on deck and capture the mutineers."

Six of Magellan's men entered the cabin where Mendoza was seated. They handed him the letter. He read it carelessly.

"But this is not the reply I expected," he ex-

claimed. "Who is Magellan to give me orders?"

Instantly he was killed by the dagger thrust of one of Magellan's men. The signal to the hidden boat's crew was given, and armed sailors came pouring on deck. In a few minutes the *Victoria* was recaptured by Magellan's seamen.

The captains of the *Concepcion* and the *San Antonio* still remained defiant, and on the following night they tried to escape secretly. But Magellan had anchored his own three ships across the entrance to the bay. The *San Antonio* crashed into the *Trinidad* in the darkness. Magellan's sailors swarmed aboard her and quickly overpowered the mutinous captain and crew. That same night, the *Concepcion* was also retaken.

"I warned you I would not have mutiny in my fleet," Magellan said grimly.

One of the captains was taken ashore and beheaded. Cartagena and another man who had been a leader in the mutiny were sentenced to be marooned. When the ships departed, the two were left

on the beach, with muskets and some food but no hope of escape. They certainly died of cold and hunger within a few weeks.

With forty-eight mutineers in chains, the ships crawled southward week after week. Black cliffs lined the shore. A freezing wind whipped spray from the tops of the waves. Whenever the wind dropped, a cold white fog hid the land from sight. But some strange sense told Magellan that the straits he was seeking lay somewhere near.

One day the *Santiago* was wrecked while exploring the dangerous waters of a shallow bay. Her half-frozen crew were picked up by Magellan's other ships, and the search went on. Sometimes the weather was so bad that the ships could travel only forty miles in twenty-four hours, but Magellan examined every bay and every inlet along the coast. He took his vessel through perilous waters into the mouths of unknown rivers.

On October 21, 1520, the ships entered an enormous bay that seemed to stretch inland for miles, its surface dotted with islands. Ice-covered mountains lined its sides. A freezing wind drove snow across the water.

"Here at last is my sea passage!" shouted Magellan. "We will go through it and find the ocean that lies toward the west."

"Sir," exclaimed an officer, "our supplies are almost finished. If we go on, we will die of hunger."

"Do you expect to live forever?" Magellan demanded. "I would sooner eat my shoes than turn back now. We will go westward, across the ocean that leads to Malaya."

The passage that we know as the Straits of Magellan is 300 miles long. Magellan and his men, the first Europeans ever to see the straits, sailed slowly through them, past towering mountains and vast glaciers. They fought against fierce winds and constant squalls. Ropes were frozen. Decks were coated thick with ice. There were rocks and evil currents and deadly cold.

The terrified captain of the *San Antonio*, a man named Gomez, felt sure that Magellan was leading the fleet to destruction. He waited for a dark night. Then he turned his ship and fled eastward through the straits. Next morning only two vessels followed Magellan's *Trinidad*.

Gomez had headed back toward Spain in the *San Antonio*.

The passage through the straits ended at last. On November 28, 1520, the *Trinidad* reached a place where the channel widened. Magellan clutched the

rail and stared eagerly at the open sea ahead. He had succeeded! Before him lay the ocean he had been determined to find.

The ships sailed north as quickly as possible. Magellan's men were eager to escape from the southern cold.

The weather soon began to improve. Flying fish skimmed across the warm blue sea. The sailors took off heavy jerseys and leather sea boots. They sprawled lazily on the sunny decks.

When the ships were about fifteen hundred miles north of the straits, Magellan turned westward across the unknown ocean. He had no idea how long it would take his ships to cross this *Mar Pacifico* (Peaceful Sea). He was well aware of how little food was left.

Day after day the voyage went on. December ended and the year 1521 arrived. A mild but steady breeze drove the ships across the ocean, but the horizon remained empty. Not a single island had been sighted. And now the food was almost gone.

"We ate powder of biscuits swarming with worms," wrote one of Magellan's officers. "We drank water that was thick with yellow slime and had been rotten for days. Men caught rats and sold them for food at five dollars each."

Then came the illness called scurvy, caused by lack of fresh fruit and vegetables. Men's ankles swelled enormously. Their gums became painful and their teeth dropped out. One man in every twenty died.

The ships were beginning to leak. Sick and starving men had to toil at the pumps. But Magellan kept his face turned toward the west. Somewhere yonder lay the East Indies. He would reach them if he had to sail the *Trinidad* by himself. And on deck his seamen groaned and died.

"Soon we will sight land," Magellan wrote in his diary. "My men die fast, but we are approaching the East Indies at fair speed. We have not had to alter our sails during the past seventy-three days. I

know that this ocean can be crossed. I know that a ship can sail around the world. But God help us in our sufferings."

Even the rats were starving now, and there were few of them left. The sailors ate boots and leather straps. They cut up planks and swallowed the sawdust.

On March 6, 1521, the exhausted lookout in the *Trinidad's* masthead thought he saw something. He clutched a rope and staggered to his feet to peer ahead. "Land!" he screamed, and began hammering the clapper of the great copper bell beside him.

Along the horizon appeared a cluster of islands. As the ships drew nearer, the men were frantic with joy. They could see yellow beaches, flowers waving in the sunshine, streams running through grassy little valleys.

Dark-skinned natives were gathering in excited groups on the shore. Jumping into their canoes, they came paddling out to the anchored ships and swarmed aboard. They stole everything they could lay hands on and ran off with their loot. It is easy to see why those islands were named the Ladrones, or Robber Islands. Oars and knives, buckets and ropes, disappeared like magic. The half-dead seamen finally managed to drive off the thieves, and the *Trinidad's* guns fired a couple of shots. The natives fled in terror into the forests, and the sailors rowed ashore to a suddenly deserted village.

They found bananas, which they thought were figs, and ate them hungrily. They slashed open green coconuts and gulped the contents. They fell down beside the streams and drank, with their faces plunged in the water. They tore up handfuls of young grass and gnawed the sap-filled stems.

One group of seamen captured a pig, and others cut down growing sugar cane. Seven natives who tried to interfere were killed. Vast loads of bananas and coconuts and dried flying fish were taken to the ships.

Next morning, Magellan gave the order to sail. His three ships were in bad shape, and he wanted to

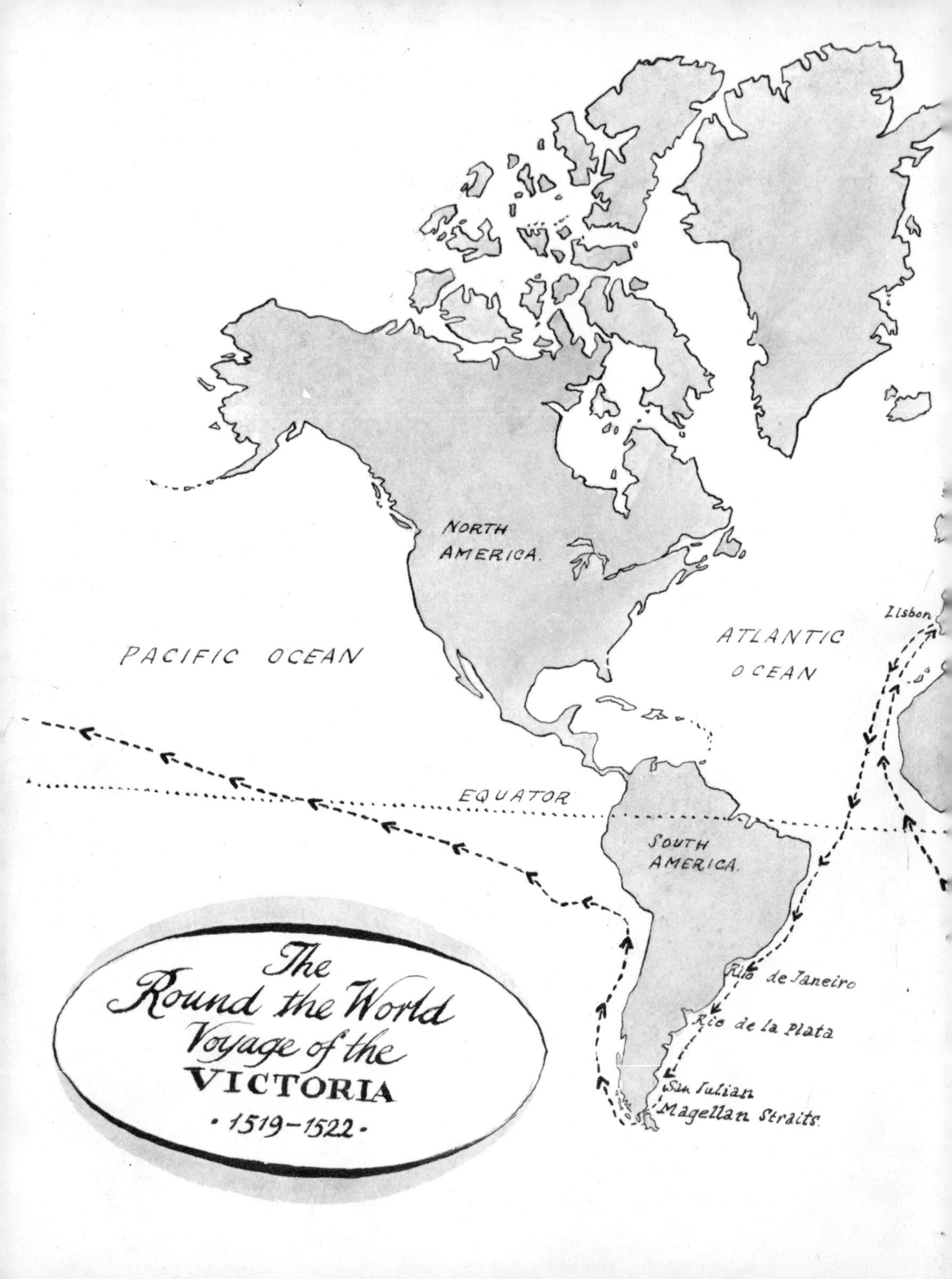
NORTH AMERICA.
PACIFIC OCEAN
ATLANTIC OCEAN
Lisbon
EQUATOR
SOUTH AMERICA.
Rio de Janeiro
Rio de la Plata
San Julian
Magellan Straits
The Round the World Voyage of the VICTORIA
· 1519–1522 ·

EUROPE
ASIA
JAPAN
CHINA
ARABIA
INDIA
RICA
Ladrones
Philippine
Islands
Calicut
Cochin
MALAYA
Cebu
Malacca
Ceylon
Borneo
INDIAN
OCEAN
Sumatra
Papua
Java
AUSTRALIA
NEW ZEALAND

finish the voyage before they sank beneath his feet.

More islands were sighted nine days later. Magellan had reached the Philippines. One of these islands was uninhabited but covered with trees. There were springs of fresh water in the valleys. Magellan ordered the sick men to be carried ashore, where tents were put up to serve as a hospital.

Magellan went from one man to another, giving them fresh fruit to eat and cool water to drink. "Our troubles are over," he told them. "We have crossed the Pacific. Now we are close to the East Indies. God willing, I shall find the way from here to Malaya."

Magellan reckoned that the Malayan port of Malacca lay to the southwest, and on March 25, 1521, he set sail in that direction. Now there were islands all along the horizon. Natives came in canoes to stare at the ships as they sailed by.

Magellan remembered a certain man in his crew called Malacca Henry, who had come to Spain from Malacca years before. He sent for him. "Speak to

those natives in the canoes in your own language," Magellan ordered.

Malacca Henry leaned over the rail and shouted a few words. The natives stared up at him and grinned. Eagerly they answered in the same language.

Magellan smiled. "They speak the language of the East Indies," he said. "Now we truly know that a ship can sail around the world."

Magellan decided to anchor at the island inhabited by the natives with whom Malacca Henry had talked. It was called Masaua. The local king came aboard the *Trinidad*, a brown-faced little man with a small gray beard. Magellan gave him a velvet cloak, a red hat, and some knives.

"You are my friend," said the delighted king. "Come, let us feast together in my palace."

Magellan went ashore with several officers. The palace had a thatched roof. Its floor was laid on posts far above the ground. To reach this floor, one had to climb up wobbly rope ladders.

The king provided a meal of roast pork and fried bananas, washed down with palm wine.

Magellan asked about supplies for his ships.

"I will take you to a nearby island called Cebu," said the king. "There is a good beach where you can repair your vessels. Wait until I have harvested my rice. Then we will go to Cebu together."

Magellan's ships reached the island of Cebu on April 7. It was fairly large and mountainous, and

the hills behind the town were covered with palms and broad-leafed banana trees.

The king of Cebu and his people had never seen white men before. They listened eagerly while Malacca Henry described the wonders of Spain. The king asked to come aboard the *Trinidad*.

Magellan and his officers arranged themselves on deck. The king of Cebu stared in amazement at suits of armor and steel swords. He examined the

red velvet chair in which Magellan was seated. He listened while the trumpets sounded a call and he admired their shining brass. Bewildered, he looked at the muzzles of iron cannon projecting from the sides of the ship.

"Your interpreter spoke the truth," he said finally. "I see that my people are not like you men of Spain. What is this wisdom which you possess?"

"We worship the true God," Magellan replied.

"Tell us about your religion," said the king. "We will listen eagerly."

Magellan and the king became good friends. All the king's officers were given knives and red caps and brightly painted beads. To the king himself, Magellan gave a crystal drinking cup.

"It is the most beautiful thing I have seen," said the king. "I am sad that I can give you nothing except rice and goats, fowls and pigs."

"We did not come to seek presents," Magellan answered, "nor did we come to trade with you. That is why I have forbidden my men to take gold from your people."

The natives of Cebu were anxious to become Christians. They came in hundreds, asking to be baptized. Magellan's sailors erected a wooden cross in the town square. A platform covered with a red carpet was set up beside it. There the king came to be baptized, followed by his younger brothers. Then came the young and beautiful queen of Cebu. She was clad from head to foot in a black and white

robe. Her lips and fingernails were painted red. On her head she wore a wide, graceful hat woven from palm leaves.

A day or so later, the king came to see Magellan. "I have ordered all my people to become Christians," he said, "and they will obey gladly. But one thing troubles me. Not far from here is an island ruled by a chieftain named Chilapulapu. He refuses to be baptized, and he has sent a message saying that he will bring his men to kill the people here who have become Christians. What shall I do?"

"I will send a message to Chilapulapu," replied

Magellan. "I will say we have no wish to harm him, but that he must leave your people alone. Otherwise we will destroy him."

Back came an impudent answer: "We, too, have spears and fighting men."

"You are my friends," Magellan said to the king of Cebu. "I will not let Chilapulapu harm you. We will attack him and teach him a lesson."

A white coral reef surrounded the chieftain's island, so Magellan's ships could not anchor near the shore. At dawn on April 27, Magellan ordered boats to be lowered. He went with forty-nine men through the reef and onto the beach. They drew their swords and prepared to fight.

Chilapulapu's village lay in a grove of palm trees. Out from the huts came hordes of half-naked warriors carrying bone-tipped spears and heavy wooden clubs. Some were armed with knives made from sharks' teeth.

Hundreds of them charged fiercely down upon the beach. Magellan had not dreamed of having to fight so many men, but now it was too late to retreat.

The sailors formed a circle and beat off the first attack. The natives paused, then made a second charge. Whirling clubs met bright steel swords. Wooden spears clattered against helmets. One Spaniard fell dead, killed by a knife thrust between the plates of his armor. A second, third, and fourth fell beside him. The warriors were attacking even more fiercely now.

"Get back to the boats," Magellan shouted.

The Spaniards began to fight their way to the beach, while Magellan himself and six others stayed to cover their retreat. A poisoned arrow struck Magellan in the leg. He pulled it out and went on fighting. A spear knocked off his helmet. He stooped and snatched it up.

"Try to get to the boats," he cried to the six men who had stayed with him. "Keep facing the enemy and fight as you go."

But retreat was impossible now. A yelling mass of warriors surrounded Magellan and his men.

Spears and clubs and daggers rained blows on them without ceasing.

Magellan's helmet was again knocked off. As he picked it up, a warrior rushed forward and struck with his spear. Magellan dodged the blow and lunged with his sword. The blade pierced the man's chest and stuck there. Magellan tried to draw his dagger. The weapon jammed in its scabbard.

The howling warriors closed in. Only two of the little group of Spaniards escaped alive. Magellan and four companions died on the beach. The date was April 27, 1521.

On September 8, 1522, a battered little ship reached Seville. She was the *Victoria*. Of the five ships that had sailed three years before, only the *Victoria* ever came home to Spain.

Eighteen seamen walked down the gangway to the quay. Their skins were almost black from tropical sunshine. Some of them were toothless from scurvy.

"We are Magellan's men," the leader told the staring crowd. "We crossed the Pacific Ocean and reached the East Indies. Our captain died there. Then we sailed home past India and South Africa. Look at us! We are the living proof that Captain Magellan was right. He always said that it would be possible to sail all the way around the world."